# This book belongs to:

_____

I am _____ years old.

Today's date:

_____

My Book of Daily Bible Verses
Level 1

A children's book produced by
The Bible Tells Me So Press

PUBLISHED BY
THE BIBLE TELLS ME SO CORPORATION
2111 W. CRESCENT AVE, SUITE C, ANAHEIM, CA 92801
WWW.THEBIBLETELLSMESO.COM

First Printing August, 2019

# My Book of Daily Bible Verses
## Level 1

The Bible Tells Me So Press

# A note to parents:

The purpose of this book is to help you to have a simple and encouraging time with your children every day in the word of God (Deuteronomy 11:18-21).

We encourage you to read these verses to your children at a consistent time on a daily basis (for example: in the morning or before going to bed). As you read them to your children they will surely have questions about what a particular word means, or what a verse as a whole may mean. This can lead to many precious short talks with your children about the verse. It is best however, not to use these times for lengthy lessons but for very simple, brief, and pleasant little chats with your child. In some cases you may be able to apply the verse in a simple way to something that happened that day. Five to eight minutes of such encouraging conversation about the verse will leave your child feeling peaceful, happy, and cherished by you and by the words of the Bible. Keeping these times brief and positive will also help them look forward to these intimate times with you every day.

You will find that this book is divided into parts, or "goals." Each part covers eight weeks, with the final part covering only four. At the beginning of each part you can set a prize or reward that you and your child (or your family) will enjoy together after that goal is reached (for example: going out for an ice-cream, or taking a family outing together). Then, as you reach each goal, you can cut out the Certificate of Completion for that goal and hang it up on the wall in your child's room. Or you can leave it in the book, whichever your child prefers.

Through this kind of daily time in the Word, children can develop a Bible-reading habit and a life-long love for God's word. The words they receive in their youth will be profitable to teach, convict, correct, and instruct them in righteousness, that they would eventually be complete and fully equipped for every good work (2 Timothy 3:14:17).

# Reward Agreement

## for finishing your
## FIRST GOAL!

As a reward for finishing your
first goal of 56 verses,
we will do the following:

_____

_____


Put the date that you started
working toward this goal below:

_____

# Verses for *Week 1*

○ **Day 1**
**Psalm 127:3**
Behold, children are the heritage of Jehovah, the fruit of the womb a reward.

○ **Day 2**
**Genesis 1:1**
In the beginning God created the heavens and the earth.

○ **Day 3**
**Job 26:7**
He stretches out the north over the void; He hangs the earth upon nothing.

○ **Day 4**
**Genesis 1:26a**
And God said, Let Us make man in Our image, according to Our likeness.

○ **Day 5**
**Genesis 1:27**
And God created man in His own image; in the image of God He created him; male and female He created them.

○ **Day 6**
**Psalm 119:73a**
Your hands have made me and fashioned me.

○ **Day 7**
**Psalm 139:13**
For it was You who formed my inward parts; You wove me together in my mother's womb.

# Verses for *Week 2*

**Psalm 139:16**

Your eyes saw my unformed substance;
and in Your book all of them were written:
The days that were ordained for me, when
not one of them was yet.

**Day 8** ◯

&#10087;

---

**Jeremiah 1:5a**

Before I formed you in the womb,
I knew you.

**Day 9** ◯

&#10087;

---

**Ephesians 6:1**

Children, obey your parents in the Lord,
for this is right.

**Day 10** ◯

&#10087;

---

**Proverbs 22:6**

Train up a child according to the way
he should go; even when he is old,
he will not depart from it.

**Day 11** ◯

&#10087;

---

**Isaiah 54:13**

And all your children will be taught of
Jehovah, and the peace of your
children will be great.

**Day 12** ◯

&#10087;

---

**Ezekiel 34:26b**

I will cause the showers to come down
in their season; there will be showers
of blessing.

**Day 13** ◯

&#10087;

---

**Isaiah 41:10a**

Do not be afraid, for I am with you.

**Day 14** ◯

# Verses for *Week 3*

**Day 15**
○

**Proverbs 15:3**
The eyes of Jehovah are in every place,
keeping watch on the evil and the good.

**Day 16**
○

**Psalm 17:8**
Guard me like the pupil of Your eye;
in the shadow of Your wings hide me.

**Day 17**
○

**Jeremiah 27:5a**
It is I who made the earth, and the people
and the animals who are on
the face of the earth.

**Day 18**
○

**2 Chronicles 15:7**
But you be strong and do not let
your hands fail, for there is reward
for your labor.

**Day 19**
○

**Colossians 3:20**
Children, obey your parents in all things,
for this is well pleasing in the Lord.

**Day 20**
○

**Proverbs 11:13**
He who goes about as a gossip reveals
secrets, but he who is of a faithful spirit
conceals a matter.

**Day 21**
○

**Isaiah 50:5**
The Lord Jehovah has opened my ear;
and I was not rebellious,
nor did I turn back.

# Verses for *Week 4*

**Proverbs 14:23**

In all labor there is profit,
but mere talk leads only to poverty.

**Day 22** ○

**Ecclesiastes 5:5**

It is better that you do not vow
than that you vow and not pay.

**Day 23** ○

**Habakkuk 2:4a**

See, he who is puffed up,
his soul is not upright within him.

**Day 24** ○

**Ephesians 4:32a**

And be kind to one another, tenderhearted,
forgiving one another.

**Day 25** ○

**Psalm 139:14**

I will praise You, for I am awesomely
and wonderfully made; Your works are
wonderful, and my soul knows it well.

**Day 26** ○

**Psalm 136:1**

Give thanks to Jehovah, for He is good;
for His lovingkindness is forever.

**Day 27** ○

**1 Thessalonians 5:18a**

In everything give thanks.

**Day 28** ○

# Verses for *Week 5*

**Day**
**29** Numbers 6:24
Jehovah bless you and keep you.

**Day**
**30** Proverbs 14:16a
A wise man fears and departs from evil.

**Day**
**31** Exodus 20:7a
You shall not take the name
of Jehovah your God in vain.

**Day**
**32** Genesis 6:9b
Noah was a righteous man, blameless in
his generations; and Noah walked with
God.

**Day**
**33** 3 John 11a
Beloved, do not imitate the evil,
but the good.

**Day**
**34** Isaiah 58:2a
Yet they seek Me day by day and
take delight in knowing My ways.

**Day**
**35** Proverbs 13:20
He who walks with wise men will be wise,
but the companion of fools will be troubled.

# Verses for *Week 6*

**Proverbs 15:18**

**Day 36** ○

A wrathful man stirs up contention,
but he who is slow to anger quiets strife.

**Psalm 14:1a**

**Day 37** ○

The fool has said in his heart,
There is no God.

**Proverbs 23:15**

**Day 38** ○

My son, if your heart is wise, my own heart
will also rejoice.

**Proverbs 12:10**

**Day 39** ○

A righteous man regards the life of his
beast, but the inward parts of the wicked
are cruel.

**Genesis 24:18**

**Day 40** ○

And [Rebekah] said, Drink, my lord. And
she hurried and lowered her pitcher on her
hand and gave [Eliezer] a drink.

**Genesis 24:19**

**Day 41** ○

And when [Rebekah] had finished giving
him a drink, she said, I will draw water for
your camels also, until they have finished
drinking.

**Genesis 24:20**

**Day 42** ○

And [Rebekah] hurried and emptied her
pitcher into the trough and ran again to
the well to draw water, and she drew it for
all his camels.

# Verses for *Week 7*

**Day 43** ✓
**Proverbs 15:25a**
Jehovah will tear down the house of the proud.

**Day 44**
**Isaiah 66:1a**
Thus says Jehovah, Heaven is My throne, and the earth the footstool for My feet.

**Day 45**
**Jeremiah 10:12**
It is He who made the earth by His power, who established the world by His wisdom, and by His understanding He stretched out the heavens.

**Day 46**
**Proverbs 1:10**
My son, if sinners entice you, do not consent.

**Day 47**
**Proverbs 11:16a**
A gracious woman lays hold of honor.

**Day 48**
**Proverbs 24:26**
He who gives an honest answer kisses the lips.

**Day 49**
**Proverbs 4:5**
Get wisdom; get understanding; do not forget nor turn away from the words of my mouth.

# Verses for *Week 8*

**Isaiah 12:4b**

Give thanks to Jehovah.

**Day**
**50** ○

---

**Isaiah 40:8**

The grass withers and the flower fades,
but the word of our God will stand forever.

**Day**
**51** ○

---

**Exodus 20:15**

You shall not steal.

**Day**
**52** ○

---

**Genesis 8:1a**

And God remembered Noah and all the
animals and all the cattle that were with
him in the ark.

**Day**
**53** ○

---

**Psalm 104:21**

The young lions roar after their prey,
even to seek their food from God.

**Day**
**54** ○

---

**Proverbs 11:21**

Be assured: The evil man will not go
unpunished; but the seed of the righteous
will be delivered.

**Day**
**55** ○

---

**Proverbs 1:5a**

That the wise man may hear and increase
in learning.

**Day**
**56** ○

# Congratulations!

You have completed 56 verses to reach

**goal number:**

1

Date Completed: _____

A Parent's Signature: _____

# Reward Agreement

## for finishing your
# SECOND GOAL!

As a reward for finishing your
second goal of the next 56 verses,
we will do the following:

_____

_____

Put the date that you started
working toward this goal below:

_____

# Verses for *Week 9*

**Day**
## 57
**Matthew 5:3**
Blessed are the poor in spirit,
for theirs is the kingdom of the heavens.

**Day**
## 58
**Matthew 5:4**
Blessed are those who mourn,
for they shall be comforted.

**Day**
## 59
**Matthew 5:5**
Blessed are the meek,
for they shall inherit the earth.

**Day**
## 60
**Matthew 5:6**
Blessed are those who hunger and thirst
for righteousness, for they
shall be satisfied.

**Day**
## 61
**Matthew 5:7**
Blessed are the merciful,
for they shall be shown mercy.

**Day**
## 62
**Matthew 5:8**
Blessed are the pure in heart,
for they shall see God.

**Day**
## 63
**Matthew 5:9**
Blessed are the peacemakers,
for they shall be called the sons of God.

# Verses for *Week 10*

**Matthew 5:10**
Blessed are those who are persecuted for
the sake of righteousness, for theirs is the
kingdom of the heavens.

**Day 64** ◯

~

**Exodus 20:3**
You shall have no other gods before Me.

**Day 65** ◯

~

**Proverbs 22:29a**
Do you see a man skilled in his work?
He will stand before kings.

**Day 66** ◯

~

**Matthew 6:26**
Look at the birds of heaven. They do not
sow nor reap nor gather into barns, yet
your heavenly Father nourishes them. Are
you not of more value than they?

**Day 67** ◯

~

**Proverbs 13:18**
Poverty and shame will come to him who
refuses correction, but he who regards
reproof will be honored.

**Day 68** ◯

~

**Proverbs 18:8**
The words of a whisperer are like dainty
morsels, and they go down into the
innermost parts of one's being.

**Day 69** ◯

~

**Proverbs 16:28**
A perverse man spreads strife,
and a whisperer separates close friends.

**Day 70** ◯

# Verses for *Week 11*

**Day 71** — Jeremiah 5:24b
Let us now fear Jehovah our God,
who gives us rain... in its season,
who preserves the appointed weeks of
the harvest for us.

**Day 72** — Proverbs 17:6
Grandchildren are the crown of old men,
and the glory of children is their fathers.

**Day 73** — Jeremiah 32:33b
Althoughy I taught them, rising up early
and teaching; but they would not listen
so as to receive instruction.

**Day 74** — Proverbs 11:14
Where no sound counsel is, the people fall;
but in the multitude of counselors
there is safety.

**Day 75** — Job 2:3b
A perfect and upright man, who fears God
and turns away from evil.

**Day 76** — Proverbs 1:7a
The fear of Jehovah is the beginning
of knowledge.

**Day 77** — Proverbs 3:5
Trust in Jehovah with all your heart, and
do not rely on your own understanding.

# Verses for *Week 12*

**Luke 6:36**

**Day 78**  ◯

Be full of compassion, even as your Father also is full of compassion.

❧

**Luke 6:38a**

**Day 79**  ◯

Give, and it will be given to you; a good measure, pressed down, shaken together, and running over, they will give into your bosom.

❧

**Luke 6:38b**

**Day 80**  ◯

For with what measure you measure, it shall be measured to you in return.

❧

**Proverbs 11:25**

**Day 81**  ◯

The blessing soul will prosper, and he who waters will also be watered himself.

❧

**Proverbs 1:8**

**Day 82**  ◯

Hear, my son, the instruction of your father, and do not reject the teaching of your mother.

❧

**Matthew 10:24**

**Day 83**  ◯

A disciple is not above the teacher, nor a slave above his master.

❧

**Luke 11:28**

**Day 84**  ◯

But He said, Blessed rather are those who hear the word of God and keep it.

# Verses for *Week 13*

**Day 85**

**Mark 9:35b**
If anyone wants to be first, he shall be the last of all and the servant of all.

**Day 86**

**Matthew 19:14a**
But Jesus said, Allow the little children and do not prevent them from coming to Me.

**Day 87**

**Proverbs 18:10**
The name of Jehovah is a strong tower; the righteous man runs into it and is safe.

**Day 88**

**Proverbs 20:11**
Even a child makes himself known by his deeds, whether his work is pure and whether it is upright.

**Day 89**

**Philippians 2:14**
Do all things without murmurings and reasonings.

**Day 90**

**Proverbs 12:16**
A fool's anger is known at once, but a prudent man conceals shame.

**Day 91**

**Proverbs 12:18**
There is one who speaks rashly like the piercings of a sword, but the tongue of the wise brings healing.

# Verses for *Week 14*

**Psalm 5:6**
**Day**
**92** ○

You will destroy those who speak lies. Jehovah abhors a man of bloodshed and deceit.

෨

**Psalm 28:7a**
**Day**
**93** ○

Jehovah is my strength and my shield; my heart trusts in Him, and I am helped.

෨

**Psalm 28:7b**
**Day**
**94** ○

Therefore my heart exults; and with my song do I give thanks to Him.

෨

**Proverbs 10:27**
**Day**
**95** ○

The fear of Jehovah prolongs days, but the years of the wicked will be shortened.

෨

**Proverbs 17:3**
**Day**
**96** ○

The refining pot is for silver and the furnace for gold, but Jehovah tries the hearts.

෨

**1 Samuel 16:7b**
**Day**
**97** ○

For it is not how man sees that matters; for man looks on the outward appearance, but Jehovah looks on the heart.

෨

**Acts 13:22b**
**Day**
**98** ○

[God] said, I have found David, the son of Jesse, a man according to My heart, who will do all My will.

# Verses for *Week 15*

**Day**
**99** ○
**Proverbs 20:22**
Do not say, I will recompense evil;
wait for Jehovah, and He will save you.

**Day**
**100** ○
**Proverbs 29:18**
Where there is no vision, the people cast
off restraint; but happy is he who
keeps the law.

**Day**
**101** ○
**Proverbs 4:27**
Do not turn to the right or to the left;
turn your foot away from evil.

**Day**
**102** ○
**Luke 8:17**
For nothing is hidden which shall not
become manifest, nor concealed which
shall not by all means be made known
and come into the open.

**Day**
**103** ○
**Proverbs 12:4a**
A worthy woman is the crown
of her husband.

**Day**
**104** ○
**Proverbs 11:22**
Like a nose-ring of gold in a pig's snout,
so is a beautiful woman who is
without discretion.

**Day**
**105** ○
**Proverbs 3:7**
Do not be wise in your own eyes;
fear Jehovah, and depart from evil.

# Verses for *Week 16*

**Proverbs 15:20** — **Day 106** ○

A wise son makes a father glad,
but a foolish man despises his mother.

꙳ ⸻⸻⸻⸻⸻⸻

**Genesis 6:22** — **Day 107** ○

And Noah did this; according to all
that God commanded him, so he did.

꙳ ⸻⸻⸻⸻⸻⸻

**1 Peter 2:13a** — **Day 108** ○

Be subject to every human institution
for the Lord's sake.

꙳ ⸻⸻⸻⸻⸻⸻

**1 Peter 2:17** — **Day 109** ○

Honor all men. Love the brotherhood.
Fear God. Honor the king.

꙳ ⸻⸻⸻⸻⸻⸻

**1 Peter 3:3** — **Day 110** ○

Let your adorning not be the outward
plaiting of hair and putting on of gold
or clothing with garments.

꙳ ⸻⸻⸻⸻⸻⸻

**1 Peter 3:4** — **Day 111** ○

But the hidden man of the heart in the
incorruptible adornment of a meek and
quiet spirit, which is very costly in the
sight of God.

꙳ ⸻⸻⸻⸻⸻⸻

**1 Peter 3:10** — **Day 112** ○

For "he who desires to love life
and see good days, let him cause his
tongue to cease from evil and his lips
to speak no guile.

The Bible Tells Me So.com

# Congratulations!

You have completed 112 verses to reach

**goal number:**

2

Date Completed: _____

A Parent's Signature: _____

# Reward Agreement

## for finishing your
# THIRD GOAL!

As a reward for finishing your
third goal of the next 56 verses,
we will do the following:

_____

_____

Put the date that you started
working toward this goal below:

_____

# Verses for *Week 17*

**Day**
**113**  ○
**1 Peter 3:11**
And let him turn away from evil and do good; let him seek peace and pursue it.

**Day**
**114**  ○
**1 Peter 3:14**
But even if you suffer because of righteousness, you are blessed.

**Day**
**115**  ○
**1 Peter 4:9**
Be hospitable to one another without murmuring.

**Day**
**116**  ○
**1 John 2:1a**
My little children, these things I write to you that you may not sin.

**Day**
**117**  ○
**3 John 4**
I have no greater joy than these things, that I hear that my children are walking in the truth.

**Day**
**118**  ○
**John 15:16a**
You did not choose Me, but I chose you.

**Day**
**119**  ○
**Exodus 20:12a**
Honor your father and your mother.

# Verses for *Week 18*

**Proverbs 26:14**

**Day 120** ○

As the door turns upon its hinges,
so does the sluggard upon his bed.

❧

**Proverbs 6:9**

**Day 121** ○

How long, sluggard, will you lie there?
When will you arise from your sleep?

❧

**Proverbs 13:4**

**Day 122** ○

The soul of the sluggard desires
and has nothing, but the soul of the diligent
will be made fat.

❧

**Proverbs 15:19**

**Day 123** ○

The way of the sluggard is like a hedge of
thorns, but the path of the upright
is paved.

❧

**Proverbs 21:25**

**Day 124** ○

The desire of the sluggard puts him
to death, for his hands refuse to work.

❧

**Proverbs 24:30-31a**

**Day 125** ○

I passed by the field of the sluggard, and
by the vineyard of the man lacking sense
31 and there it was, all overgrown with
thorns.

❧

**Proverbs 24:33-34**

**Day 126** ○

A little sleep, a little slumber, a little
folding of the hands to rest, 34 and your
poverty will come upon you like a robber,
and your want, like an armed man.

# Verses for *Week 19*

**Day**
## 127
**Proverbs 6:6**
Go to the ant, you sluggard;
consider its ways, and be wise.

**Day**
## 128
**Proverbs 19:24**
The sluggard buries his hand in the dish,
and will not even bring it back
to his mouth.

**Day**
## 129
**Luke 18:14b**
For everyone who exalts himself shall
be humbled, but he who humbles himself
shall be exalted.

**Day**
## 130
**1 John 4:7a**
Beloved, let us love one another,
because love is of God.

**Day**
## 131
**Psalm 37:21**
The wicked borrow but do not repay,
but the righteous is gracious and gives.

**Day**
## 132
**Psalm 37:26**
He is always gracious and lends,
and his seed becomes a blessing.

**Day**
## 133
**Psalm 41:1**
Blessed is he who considers the poor; in
the day of evil Jehovah will deliver him.

# Verses for *Week 20*

**Proverbs 14:29**

**Day 134** ○

He who is slow to anger is of great understanding, but he who has a hasty spirit exalts folly.

*✑*

**Proverbs 15:1**

**Day 135** ○

A soft answer turns away anger, but a grievous word stirs up anger.

*✑*

**Proverbs 19:11**

**Day 136** ○

The discretion of a man makes him slow to anger, and it is his glory to overlook a transgression.

*✑*

**Proverbs 22:24**

**Day 137** ○

Make no friendship with a man who is given to anger, and with a wrathful man do not go.

*✑*

**Proverbs 29:11**

**Day 138** ○

A fool utters all his anger, but a wise man holds it back.

*✑*

**Proverbs 14:17a**

**Day 139** ○

He who is quick to anger will deal foolishly.

*✑*

**Proverbs 25:28**

**Day 140** ○

Like a city that is broken down, without walls, is a man whose spirit is without restraint.

# Verses for *Week 21*

**Day**
**141**
**Proverbs 16:32**
He who is slow to anger is better than the
mighty; and he who rules his spirit,
than he who captures a city.

**Day**
**142**
**Job 22:27a**
You will pray to Him, and He will hear you.

**Day**
**143**
**John 15:12**
This is My commandment, that you love
one another even as I have loved you.

**Day**
**144**
**Psalm 56:11**
In God do I trust; I will not be afraid.
What can man do to me?

**Day**
**145**
**Psalm 56:3**
When I am afraid, I trust in You.

**Day**
**146**
**Malachi 3:16a**
Then those who feared Jehovah spoke to
one another, each with his neighbor.
And Jehovah gave heed and listened.

**Day**
**147**
**Joshua 2:11b**
For Jehovah your God, He is God
in heaven above and upon earth beneath.

# Verses for *Week 22*

**Proverbs 21:24**

Proud, Haughty, Scorner are the names of him who works in the arrogance of pride.

**Day 148** ○

❧

**1 Corinthians 14:40**

But all things must be done becomingly and in order.

**Day 149** ○

❧

**Psalm 16:8**

I have set Jehovah before me continually; because He is at my right hand, I shall not be shaken.

**Day 150** ○

❧

**Jeremiah 31:34b**

For all of them will know Me, from the little one among them even to the great one among them, declares Jehovah.

**Day 151** ○

❧

**Psalm 92:1**

It is good to give thanks to Jehovah and to sing psalms to Your name, O Most High.

**Day 152** ○

❧

**Psalm 34:2**

My soul makes its boast in Jehovah; the lowly hear and they rejoice.

**Day 153** ○

❧

**Luke 18:16b**

Allow the little children to come to Me, and do not forbid them, for of such is the kingdom of God.

**Day 154** ○

# Verses for *Week 23*

**Day**
## 155
**Luke 6:31**
And just as you want men to do to you, do to them likewise.

**Day**
## 156
**Luke 6:35a**
But love your enemies, and do good and lend, expecting nothing in return, and your reward will be great.

**Day**
## 157
**1 Peter 5:5a**
In like manner, younger men, be subject to elders.

**Day**
## 158
**1 Peter 5:5b**
And all of you, gird yourselves with humility toward one another.

**Day**
## 159
**1 Peter 5:5c**
Because God resists the proud but gives grace to the humble.

**Day**
## 160
**Proverbs 29:23**
A man's pride will bring him low, but he who is of a lowly spirit will obtain honor.

**Day**
## 161
**Proverbs 13:10a**
Through pride comes nothing but strife.

# Verses for *Week 24*

**Proverbs 16:18**

**Day 162** ◯

Pride goes before destruction,
and a haughty spirit before a fall.

❧

**Proverbs 21:23**

**Day 163** ◯

Whoever guards his mouth and his tongue
keeps his soul from troubles.

❧

**James 3:5**

**Day 164** ◯

So also the tongue is a little member
yet boasts great things. Behold,
how great a forest so little a fire ignites!

❧

**James 3:10**

**Day 165** ◯

Out of the same mouth come forth blessing
and cursing. These things, my brothers,
ought not to be so.

❧

**Proverbs 29:20**

**Day 166** ◯

Do you see a man who is hasty in his
words? There is more hope for a fool
than for him.

❧

**Proverbs 25:11**

**Day 167** ◯

A word fitly spoken is like apples of gold
in settings of silver.

❧

**Proverbs 4:24**

**Day 168** ◯

Put away from you crooked speech,
and put perverse talk far from you.

The Bible Tells Me So.com

# Congratulations!

You have completed 168 verses to reach **goal number:**

3

Date Completed: _____

A Parent's Signature: _____

# *Reward Agreement*

### for finishing your
# FOURTH GOAL!

As a reward for finishing your
fourth goal of the next 56 verses,
we will do the following:

_____

_____

Put the date that you started
working toward this goal below:

_____

# Verses for *Week 25*

**Day**
## 169
**Colossians 4:6**
Let your speech be always with grace, seasoned with salt, that you may know how you ought to answer each one.

**Day**
## 170
**Proverbs 10:10**
He who winks with the eye causes grief, and the foolish in speech will be cast down.

**Day**
## 171
**Proverbs 26:18-19**
Like a madman who shoots firebrands, arrows, and death, [19] so is the man who deceives his neighbor, and says, Was I not joking?

**Day**
## 172
**1 John 3:18**
Little children, let us not love in word nor in tongue but in deed and truthfulness.

**Day**
## 173
**Proverbs 30:5**
Every word of God is tried; He is a shield to those who take refuge in Him.

**Day**
## 174
**Psalm 119:105**
Your word is a lamp to my feet and a light to my path.

**Day**
## 175
**Psalm 33:6**
By the word of Jehovah the heavens were made, and all their host, by the breath of His mouth.

# Verses for *Week 26*

**1 Chronicles 16:34**
Give thanks to Jehovah, for He is good,
for His lovingkindness is forever.

**Day 176** ◯

**Proverbs 17:20**
He who has a crooked heart finds no good,
and he who has a perverse tongue
falls into evil.

**Day 177** ◯

**Exodus 20:17a**
You shall not covet...

**Day 178** ◯

**Romans 13:3b**
Do you want to have no fear of the
authority? Do what is good, and you will
have praise from him.

**Day 179** ◯

**Romans 13:5**
Therefore it is necessary to be subject,
not only because of wrath but also because
of conscience.

**Day 180** ◯

**Romans 13:7**
Render to all the things due: tax to whom
tax is due, custom to whom custom is due,
fear to whom fear is due, honor to whom
honor is due.

**Day 181** ◯

**Proverbs 19:15**
Slothfulness casts into a deep sleep,
and the idle soul will suffer hunger.

**Day 182** ◯

# Verses for *Week 27*

**Day 183** ✓

**Proverbs 19:5**
A false witness will not go unpunished, and he who utters lies will not escape.

**Day 184**

**Isaiah 29:15**
Woe to those who hide deeply their counsel from Jehovah, and whose deeds are in the dark and who say, Who sees us? And, Who knows us?

**Day 185**

**Isaiah 29:16a**
You turn things upside down! Shall the potter be considered to be like the clay?

**Day 186**

**Proverbs 26:20**
For lack of wood the fire goes out, and where there is no whisperer, contention quiets down.

**Day 187**

**Proverbs 24:28b**
And do not deceive with your lips.

**Day 188**

**Proverbs 30:32**
If you have been foolish in exalting yourself, or if you have thought an evil scheme, put your hand upon your mouth.

**Day 189**

**James 5:12b**
Do not swear, neither by heaven nor by earth nor with any other oath; but let your yes be yes, and your no, no, lest you fall under judgment.

# Verses for *Week 28*

**Proverbs 20:19** — **Day 190** ○

He who goes about as a gossip reveals secrets; therefore do not associate with one who opens his lips wide.

**Psalm 46:10** — **Day 191** ○

Be still and know that I am God. I will be exalted among the nations; I will be exalted on earth.

**Proverbs 6:12** — **Day 192** ○

A worthless man, a wicked man, goes around with a perverse mouth.

**Proverbs 23:16** — **Day 193** ○

My inward parts will also exult, when your lips speak right things.

**Proverbs 27:4** — **Day 194** ○

Wrath is cruel, and anger is overwhelming, but who can stand before jealousy?

**James 3:16** — **Day 195** ○

For where jealousy and selfish ambition are, there disorder and every worthless practice are.

**Psalm 34:13** — **Day 196** ○

Guard your tongue from evil, and your lips from speaking deceit.

# Verses for *Week 29*

### Day 197
**Proverbs 12:22**
Lying lips are an abomination to Jehovah, but those who deal faithfully are His delight.

### Day 198
**Isaiah 64:8**
But now, Jehovah, You are our Father; we are the clay; and You, our Potter; and all of us are the work of Your hand.

### Day 199
**Proverbs 13:3**
He who guards his mouth keeps his soul, but he who opens wide his lips will have destruction.

### Day 200
**Proverbs 17:27a**
He who restrains his words has knowledge.

### Day 201
**Isaiah 30:23a**
Then He will give rain for your seed, which you will sow in the ground.

### Day 202
**Exodus 20:13**
You shall not kill.

### Day 203
**Isaiah 66:2a**
For all these things My hand has made, and so all these things have come into being, declares Jehovah.

# Verses for *Week 30*

**Isaiah 66:2b** **Day**
**204** ○

But to this kind of man will I look,
to him who is poor and of a contrite spirit,
and who trembles at My word.

❧ ─────────────────────────────

**1 Timothy 4:12** **Day**
**205** ○

Let no one despise your youth,
but be a pattern to the believers in word,
in conduct, in love, in faith, in purity.

❧ ─────────────────────────────

**Jeremiah 1:17b** **Day**
**206** ○

Do not be dismayed before them....

❧ ─────────────────────────────

**Jeremiah 14:22b** **Day**
**207** ○

Therefore we wait for You, for You have
made all these things.

❧ ─────────────────────────────

**Jeremiah 18:3** **Day**
**208** ○

So I went down to the potter's house,
and he was there doing work at his wheel.

❧ ─────────────────────────────

**Jeremiah 31:35a** **Day**
**209** ○

Thus says Jehovah, who gives the sun for
light by day and the order of the moon
and the stars for light by night.

❧ ─────────────────────────────

**Jeremiah 31:35b** **Day**
**210** ○

Who stirs up the sea so that its waves
roar —Jehovah of hosts is His name.

# Verses for *Week 31*

**Day**
**211**
**Proverbs 24:1**
Do not be envious of evil men,
nor desire to be with them.

**Day**
**212**
**Proverbs 24:19b**
Do not be envious of the wicked.

**Day**
**213**
**Proverbs 23:17**
Do not let your heart envy sinners,
but live in the fear of Jehovah all day long.

**Day**
**214**
**Proverbs 14:7**
Go from the presence of a foolish man,
for you will not perceive in him the lips
of knowledge.

**Day**
**215**
**1 Corinthians 15:33**
Do not be deceived: Evil companionships
corrupt good morals.

**Day**
**216**
**Proverbs 23:4**
Do not weary yourself to become rich;
cease from your consideration of it.

**Day**
**217**
**Proverbs 3:19**
Jehovah by wisdom founded the earth; He
established the heavens by understanding.

# Verses for *Week 32*

**Psalm 102:25**
### Day 218 ○
Of old You laid the foundation of the earth, and the heavens are the work of Your hands.

❧

**Psalm 90:2**
### Day 219 ○
Before the mountains were brought forth, and before You gave birth to the earth and the world, indeed from eternity to eternity, You are God.

❧

**Proverbs 16:4a**
### Day 220 ○
Jehovah has made everything for its own purpose.

❧

**Isaiah 44:24a**
### Day 221 ○
Thus says Jehovah who redeemed you and formed you from the womb.

❧

**Isaiah 44:24b**
### Day 222 ○
I am Jehovah who makes all things, who alone stretches out the heavens, who spread out the earth (Who was with Me?).

❧

**Isaiah 45:18a**
### Day 223 ○
For thus says Jehovah, who created the heavens—He is the God who formed the earth and made it.

❧

**Isaiah 45:18b**
### Day 224 ○
He established it; He did not create it waste, but He formed it to be inhabited: I am Jehovah and there is no one else.

# Congratulations!

You have completed 224 verses to reach

**goal number:**

4

Date Completed: _____

A Parent's Signature: _____

The Bible Tells Me So...com

# for finishing your
# FIFTH GOAL!

As a reward for finishing your
fifth goal of the next 56 verses,
we will do the following:

_____

_____

Put the date that you started
working toward this goal below:

_____

# Verses for *Week 33*

**Day**
**225**
**Proverbs 22:9a**
He who is generous will be blessed.

**Day**
**226**
**Proverbs 29:24a**
Whoever is partner with a thief hates
his own soul.

**Day**
**227**
**Ephesians 4:28**
He who steals should steal no more, but
rather should labor, working with his own
hands in that which is respectable, that
he may have something to share with him
who has need.

**Day**
**228**
**Proverbs 3:31**
Do not envy a man of violence,
and do not choose any of his ways.

**Day**
**229**
**Proverbs 3:12**
For whom Jehovah loves He disciplines,
even as a father, the son in whom
he delights.

**Day**
**230**
**Matthew 7:3**
And why do you look at the splinter which
is in your brother's eye, but the beam in
your eye you do not consider?

**Day**
**231**
**Proverbs 30:8**
Remove far from me falsehood and lies.
Give me neither poverty nor riches;
feed me with the food that is my portion.

# Verses for *Week 34*

**Proverbs 27:2a**

Let another praise you, and not
your own mouth.

**Day 232** ○

---

**Proverbs 4:23**

Keep your heart with all vigilance,
for from it are the issues of life.

**Day 233** ○

---

**Psalm 138:1a**

I will give You thanks with all my heart.

**Day 234** ○

---

**Psalm 15:2**

He who walks in integrity and does
righteousness and speaks truth
from his heart.

**Day 235** ○

---

**Psalm 90:12**

Teach us then to number our days
that we may gain a heart of wisdom.

**Day 236** ○

---

**2 Thessalonians 3:13**

But you, brothers, do not lose heart
in doing good.

**Day 237** ○

---

**Proverbs 21:2**

Every way of a man is right in his own
eyes, but Jehovah weighs the hearts.

**Day 238** ○

# Verses for *Week 35*

**Day**
**239**

**Proverbs 16:5**
Every one who is proud in heart is an abomination to Jehovah; be assured: He will not be unpunished.

**Day**
**240**

**Exodus 20:17a**
You shall not covet...

**Day**
**241**

**Proverbs 17:20b**
And he who has a perverse tongue falls into evil.

**Day**
**242**

**Proverbs 23:12**
Apply your heart to instruction, and your ears to words of knowledge.

**Day**
**243**

**Galatians 6:7**
Do not be deceived: God is not mocked; for whatever a man sows, this he will also reap.

**Day**
**244**

**Proverbs 28:14**
Blessed is the man who always fears, but he who hardens his heart will fall into calamity.

**Day**
**245**

**Proverbs 3:3**
Do not let lovingkindness and truth forsake you: bind them around your neck; write them upon the tablet of your heart.

# Verses for *Week 36*

**Psalm 138:1a**
**Day 246** ○
I will give You thanks with all my heart.

**Proverbs 31:30**
**Day 247** ○
Grace is deceitful, and beauty is vain;
but a woman who fears Jehovah,
she will be praised.

**Proverbs 4:14-15**
**Day 248** ○
Do not enter the path of the wicked,
and do not walk in the way of the evil.
15 Avoid it; do not pass by it; turn away
from it and pass on by.

**Psalm 10:3a**
**Day 249** ○
For the wicked man boasts of the desire
of his soul.

**Proverbs 7:4**
**Day 250** ○
Say to wisdom, You are my sister,
and call understanding your close friend.

**Proverbs 8:17**
**Day 251** ○
I love those who love me, and those who
seek me diligently will find me.

**Ecclesiastes 3:1**
**Day 252** ○
For everything there is a season, and
a time for every purpose under heaven.

# Verses for *Week 37*

**Day 253** — Psalm 119:1
Blessed are those whose way is perfect, who walk in the law of Jehovah.

**Day 254** — Proverbs 22:2
The rich and the poor have this in common: Jehovah is the maker of them all.

**Day 255** — Proverbs 29:13
The poor man and the oppressor have this in common: Jehovah gives light to the eyes of them both.

**Day 256** — Proverbs 20:12
The hearing ear and the seeing eye — Jehovah has made both of them.

**Day 257** — Psalm 112:1
Hallelujah! Blessed is the man who fears Jehovah, who delights greatly in His commandments.

**Day 258** — Psalm 118:24
This is the day that Jehovah has made; let us exult and rejoice in it.

**Day 259** — Proverbs 9:10
The fear of Jehovah is the beginning of wisdom, and the knowledge of the Holy One is understanding.

# Verses for *Week 38*

**Psalm 1:6** **Day 260** ○

For Jehovah knows the way of the righteous, but the way of the wicked will perish.

❧ ────────────────────────────

**Psalm 103:13** **Day 261** ○

As compassionate as a father is toward his children, so compassionate is Jehovah toward those who fear Him.

❧ ────────────────────────────

**Psalm 77:20** **Day 262** ○

You led Your people like a flock by the hand of Moses and Aaron.

❧ ────────────────────────────

**Proverbs 14:5** **Day 263** ○

A faithful witness will not lie, but a false witness utters lies.

❧ ────────────────────────────

**Psalm 150:6** **Day 264** ○

Let everything that has breath praise Jehovah. Hallelujah!

❧ ────────────────────────────

**Ruth 1:16b** **Day 265** ○

For wherever you go, I will go, and wherever you dwell, I will dwell; and your people will be my people, and your God will be my God.

❧ ────────────────────────────

**Proverbs 16:6b** **Day 266** ○

And by the fear of Jehovah men depart from evil.

# Verses for *Week 39*

○ **Day 267**  **Psalm 58:3**
The wicked are estranged from the womb; they err from their birth, speaking lies.

○ **Day 268**  **Ephesians 4:25a**
Therefore having put off the lie, speak truth each one with his neighbor.

○ **Day 269**  **Proverbs 20:17**
The bread of falsehood is sweet to a man, but afterward his mouth will be filled with gravel.

○ **Day 270**  **Proverbs 23:20a**
Do not be among those who get drunk with wine.

○ **Day 271**  **Proverbs 23:21a**
For the drunkard and the glutton will come to poverty.

○ **Day 272**  **Proverbs 20:1**
Wine is a mocker, strong drink a brawler; and whoever errs by it does not become wise.

○ **Day 273**  **Romans 13:1**
Let every person be subject to the authorities over him, for there is no authority except from God, and those which exist are ordained by God.

# Verses for *Week* 40

**Psalm 37:37**

Observe the perfect man, and watch the upright man; for there is a future for the man of peace.

**Day 274** ✓ ○

~

**Proverbs 21:8**

The way of a guilty man is crooked; but as for the pure, his work is right.

**Day 275** ○

~

**Proverbs 11:27**

He who diligently seeks good seeks favor; but as for him who searches after evil, it will come to him.

**Day 276** ○

~

**Colossians 3:20**

Children, obey your parents in all things, for this is well pleasing in the Lord.

**Day 277** ○

~

**Judges 2:17b**

They turned aside quickly from the way in which their fathers walked, the way of obeying the commandments of Jehovah; this they did not do.

**Day 278** ○

~

**Hebrews 13:16**

But do not forget doing good and sharing with others, for with such sacrifices God is well pleased.

**Day 279** ○

~

**Proverbs 4:13a**

Take hold of instruction; do not let go.

**Day 280** ○

*Congratulations!*

You have completed 280 verses to reach
**goal number:**

5

The Bible Tells Me So.com

Date Completed: _____

A Parent's Signature: _____

# for finishing your
# SIXTH GOAL!

As a reward for finishing your
sixth goal of the next 56 verses,
we will do the following:

_____

_____

Put the date that you started
working toward this goal below:

_____

# Verses for *Week 41*

**Day**
**281**

**Proverbs 4:18**
But the path of the righteous is like
the light of dawn, which shines brighter
and brighter until the full day.

**Day**
**282**

**Proverbs 5:21**
For the ways of a man are before the eyes
of Jehovah, and He ponders all his paths.

**Day**
**283**

**Proverbs 12:11**
He who tills his land will have plenty
of bread, but he who pursues worthless
things lacks sense.

**Day**
**284**

**Proverbs 23:24**
The father of the righteous man will
greatly exult, and he who begets a wise
child will rejoice in him.

**Day**
**285**

**1 Thessalonians 4:9b**
For you yourselves are taught of God
to love one another.

**Day**
**286**

**1 Thessalonians 5:15**
See that no one repays anyone
evil for evil, but always pursue what is
good both for one another and for all.

**Day**
**287**

**2 Timothy 3:2**
For men will be lovers of self, lovers
of money, boasters, arrogant, revilers,
disobedient to parents, unthankful, unholy.

# Verses for Week 42

**3 John 1:4**

**Day 288** ✓ ◯

I have no greater joy than these things, that I hear that my children are walking in the truth.

☙ ────────────────

**Deuteronomy 16:17**

**Day 289** ◯

Each man shall give as he is able to give, according to the blessing of Jehovah your God, which He has given you.

☙ ────────────────

**Ecclesiastes 12:14**

**Day 290** ◯

For God will bring every deed to judgment, with every secret thing, whether good or evil.

☙ ────────────────

**Ecclesiastes 12:1a**

**Day 291** ◯

Remember also your Creator in the days of your youth.

☙ ────────────────

**Ecclesiastes 4:12**

**Day 292** ◯

And while a man may prevail against the one, the two will withstand him; and a threefold cord is not quickly broken.

☙ ────────────────

**Proverbs 24:8**

**Day 293** ◯

He who devises to do evil, men will call him a mischief-maker.

☙ ────────────────

**Proverbs 25:27**

**Day 294** ◯

It is not good to eat much honey, nor is it glory for men to search out their own glory.

*MY BOOK OF DAILY BIBLE VERSES - LEVEL 1*

# Verses for *Week 43*

**Day 295** — Proverbs 27:18

Whoever tends a fig tree will eat its fruit, and he who takes care of his master will be honored.

**Day 296** — Proverbs 28:13

He who covers his transgressions will not prosper, but whoever confesses and forsakes them will obtain mercy.

**Day 297** — Proverbs 28:18

Whoever walks uprightly will be delivered, but he who is perverse in his ways will fall all at once.

**Day 298** — Proverbs 28:19

He who tills his land will have plenty of bread, but he who pursues worthless things will have plenty of poverty.

**Day 299** — Proverbs 28:20a

A faithful man will abound with blessings.

**Day 300** — Titus 2:7a

Concerning all things presenting yourself as a pattern of good works.

**Day 301** — Proverbs 29:1

He who hardens his neck after being often reproved will suddenly be broken beyond remedy.

# Verses for *Week 44*

**Proverbs 3:20**

**Day 302** ○

By His knowledge the depths were broken open and the skies drop down the dew.

❧

**Proverbs 3:34b**

**Day 303** ○

But to the humble He gives grace.

❧

**Psalm 145:9**

**Day 304** ○

Jehovah is good to all, and His compassions are upon all His works.

❧

**Matthew 18:10**

**Day 305** ○

See that you do not despise one of these little ones, for I say to you that their angels in the heavens continually behold the face of My Father who is in the heavens.

❧

**Matthew 28:20**

**Day 306** ○

Teaching them to observe all that I have commanded you. And behold, I am with you all the days until the consummation of the age.

❧

**Matthew 4:4b**

**Day 307** ○

"Man shall not live on bread alone, but on every word that proceeds out through the mouth of God."

❧

**1 Samuel 1:27**

**Day 308** ○

It was for this child that I prayed, and Jehovah has granted me my request that I requested from Him.

# Verses for *Week 45*

**Day**
## 309
**Leviticus 25:17**
And you shall not wrong one another, but you shall fear your God; for I am Jehovah your God.

**Day**
## 310
**Proverbs 10:16**
The wages of the righteous man lead to life; the income of the wicked man, to sin.

**Day**
## 311
**Proverbs 10:17**
He who heeds instruction is on the path of life, but he who forsakes reproof goes astray.

**Day**
## 312
**1 Timothy 6:10a**
For the love of money is a root of all evils.

**Day**
## 313
**Proverbs 11:27**
He who diligently seeks good seeks favor; but as for him who searches after evil, it will come to him.

**Day**
## 314
**Exodus 20:4a**
You shall not make for yourself an idol.

**Day**
## 315
**Proverbs 10:5**
He who gathers in summer is a prudent son, but he who sleeps at harvest time is a son who brings shame.

# Verses for *Week 46*

**2 Kings 22:1a**

Josiah was eight years old when he began to reign, and he reigned thirty-one years in Jerusalem.

**Day 316** ○

❧ ────────────

**2 Kings 22:2**

And [Josiah] did what was right in the eyes of Jehovah and walked in all the way of David his father and did not turn to the right or to the left.

**Day 317** ○

❧ ────────────

**2 Kings 23:25**

And before [Josiah] there was no king like him who turned to Jehovah with all his heart and with all his soul and with all his might..., and after him no one has risen up like him.

**Day 318** ○

❧ ────────────

**Proverbs 13:11**

Wealth obtained by vanity will be diminished, but he who gathers by labor increases it.

**Day 319** ○

❧ ────────────

**Proverbs 14:15**

The simple man believes every word, but the prudent man considers his steps.

**Day 320** ○

❧ ────────────

**Philippians 1:9**

And this I pray, that your love may abound yet more and more in full knowledge and all discernment.

**Day 321** ○

❧ ────────────

**Proverbs 14:31**

He who oppresses the poor reproaches his Maker, but he who is gracious to the needy honors Him.

**Day 322** ○

# Verses for *Week 47*

**Day**
## 323
**Proverbs 14:9b**
But among the upright there is good will.

**Day**
## 324
**Proverbs 15:16**
Better is a little with the fear of Jehovah than great treasure and turmoil with it.

**Day**
## 325
**Ephesians 6:2-3**
"Honor your father and mother," which is the first commandment with a promise, 3 "That it may be well with you and that you may live long on the earth."

**Day**
## 326
**Luke 2:51a**
And [Jesus] went down with [His parents] and came to Nazareth, and was subject to them.

**Day**
## 327
**Luke 2:52**
And Jesus advanced in wisdom and stature and in the grace manifested in Him before God and men.

**Day**
## 328
**Proverbs 17:17**
A friend loves at all times, and a brother is born for adversity.

**Day**
## 329
**Proverbs 15:17**
Better is a dinner of vegetables where love is than a fattened ox and hatred with it.

# Verses for *Week 48*

**Daniel 1:8a**

But Daniel set his heart not to defile himself.

**Day 330** ○

❧

**Daniel 1:19b**

And among them all none were found like Daniel, Hananiah, Mishael, and Azariah; therefore they stood in the presence of the king.

**Day 331** ○

❧

**Daniel 2:14a**

Then Daniel responded in counsel and with discretion.

**Day 332** ○

❧

**Daniel 2:28a**

But there is a God in the heavens who reveals mysteries.

**Day 333** ○

❧

**Proverbs 18:17**

The first to plead his case seems just, until his neighbor comes and cross-examines him.

**Day 334** ○

❧

**Ephesians 4:26b**

Do not let the sun go down on your indignation.

**Day 335** ○

❧

**Proverbs 18:19**

A brother offended is harder to be gained than a strong city, and contentions are like the bars of a castle.

**Day 336** ○

# Congratulations!

You have completed 336 verses to reach **goal number:**

6

Date Completed: _____

A Parent's Signature: _____

The Bible Tells Me So.com

# Reward Agreement

for finishing all

## 365 VERSES!

As a reward for finishing your
final goal of the last 29 verses
and completing the entire book,
we will do the following:

_____

_____

Put the date that you started
working toward this goal below:

_____

# Verses for *Week 49*

**Day**
**337**

Proverbs 31:10
Who can find a worthy woman?
For her price is far above corals.

**Day**
**338**

Proverbs 31:16
She considers a field and buys it; with the
fruit of her hands she plants a vineyard.

**Day**
**339**

Proverbs 31:18
She samples her merchandise to be sure it
is good; her lamp does not go out by night.

**Day**
**340**

Proverbs 31:25
Strength and dignity are her clothing,
and she happily looks forward
to the time to come.

**Day**
**341**

Proverbs 31:26
She opens her mouth with wisdom,
and the law of kindness is on her tongue.

**Day**
**342**

Proverbs 31:27
She watches closely over the ways
of her household and does not
eat the bread of idleness.

**Day**
**343**

Proverbs 31:28-29
Her children rise up and call her blessed;
her husband also, and he praises her,
saying: 29 Many daughters have done
worthily, but you surpass them all.

# Verses for *Week 50*

**Ephesians 4:29a**
**Day 344** ○

Let no corrupt word proceed out of your mouth.

❧

**Proverbs 19:18a**
**Day 345** ○

Discipline your son, for there is hope.

❧

**Proverbs 19:20**
**Day 346** ○

Listen to counsel, and receive instruction, that you may be wise at the end of your days.

❧

**Proverbs 19:22**
**Day 347** ○

What is desirable in a man is his kindness, and a poor man is better than a liar.

❧

**Proverbs 19:23a**
**Day 348** ○

The fear of Jehovah leads to life.

❧

**Proverbs 20:3**
**Day 349** ○

It is an honor for a man to keep away from strife, but every fool rushes headlong into it.

❧

**Philippians 2:4**
**Day 350** ○

Not regarding each his own virtues, but each the virtues of others also.

# Verses for *Week 51*

**Day**
## 351
**Philippians 2:14**
Do all things without murmurings
and reasonings.

**Day**
## 352
**Proverbs 23:22**
Listen to your father who begot you,
and do not despise your mother
when she is old.

**Day**
## 353
**Proverbs 23:23**
Buy truth, and do not sell it; buy wisdom
and instruction and understanding.

**Day**
## 354
**Psalm 23:1**
Jehovah is my Shepherd;
I will lack nothing.

**Day**
## 355
**Proverbs 3:6**
In all your ways acknowledge Him,
and He will make your paths straight.

**Day**
## 356
**Proverbs 30:25**
The ants are a clan without strength,
yet they prepare their food in the summer.

**Day**
## 357
**Psalm 13:6**
I will sing to Jehovah, for He has dealt
bountifully with me.

# Verses for *Week 52*

**Psalm 145:9**

Day

**358** ○ ✓

Jehovah is good to all, and His
compassions are upon all His works.

❧ ─────────────────────

**Psalm 19:1**

Day

**359** ○

The heavens declare the glory of God,
and the expanse proclaims the work
of His hands.

❧ ─────────────────────

**Psalm 34:11**

Day

**360** ○

Come, children; hear me. I will teach you
the fear of Jehovah.

❧ ─────────────────────

**Psalms 22:3**

Day

**361** ○

But You are holy, You who sit enthroned
upon the praises of Israel.

❧ ─────────────────────

**Psalm 22:9**

Day

**362** ○

But You are the One who drew me forth
from the womb, who made me trust
while at my mother's breasts.

❧ ─────────────────────

**Matthew 22:37-38**

Day

**363** ○

And He said to him, "You shall love the Lord
your God with all your heart and with all
your soul and with all your mind."
38 This is the great and first commandment.

❧ ─────────────────────

**Matthew 22:39**

Day

**364** ○

And the second is like it: "You shall love
your neighbor as yourself."

# Day
# 365

**2 Timothy 3:15a**

And that from a babe you
have known
the sacred writings.

*Congratulations!*

You have completed all

# 365

verses for level 1.

Date Completed: _____

A Parent's Signature: _____

The Bible Tells Me So.com

For more
books, videos, songs, and crafts
visit us online at
TheBibleTellsMeSo.com

**Standing on the Bible and growing!**

Made in the USA
Lexington, KY
07 November 2019